Drafts

Drafts

An Imperfect Collection Of Writing

Mark Travis Rivera

ISBN: 1546975063
ISBN-13: 9781546975069
Library of Congress Control Number: 2017910473
CreateSpace Independent Publishing Platform
North Charleston, South Carolina

Dedication

This book is dedicated to three special people in my life.

First, my niece Jailyn, who is my biggest source of joy.

Secondly, my spiritual father Anthony, who through his own writing gave me the courage to write this book.

Lastly, to Carmen Ortiz who gave me the opportunity of a lifetime. Thank you for always believing in me.

Table of Contents

Acknowledgments

There are so many people to thank for helping to make this book a reality. First and foremost I would like to thank my family—mom, my sister Jennifer, my niece Jailyn. My best friends Jennifer, Jasmine, and Shaneyce for constantly pushing me to be my best self. To Brista, thank you for always believing in me. I, of course, have to thank my editor Laurie, who without whom this book would not be possible. Thanks to Miranda for bringing my words to life through your artistic drawings. To my dear friend Alysia for writing the foreword. Special thanks to all the funders of this book, especially to my Nani and Ashley Bracey. Your financial contribution is greatly appreciated. I would also like to thank Dr. Brené Brown—your work gave me the courage to own my story and share it with the world. Lastly, I would like to thank all the men who inspired the creation of this collection. Thank you for teaching me some of the most difficult lessons about love and loss.

"Owning our story can be hard but not nearly as difficult as spending our lives running from it. Embracing our vulnerabilities is risky but not nearly as dangerous as giving up on love and belonging and joy—the experiences that make us the most vulnerable. Only when we are brave enough to explore the darkness will we discover the infinite power of our light."

— Brené Brown

Foreword

I cannot remember when or where I met Mark Travis Rivera but over the years several things have consistently shocked me about him. The first is his commitment to his word, to holding himself accountable. The second is what seems like his limitless capacity for courage and vulnerability. The third is his expanding ability to love others around him without ceasing to love himself. Most people take a mantra like "I am enough" and at best they memorize it, write it on a sticky note, or repeat it to themselves when times get tough. Mark took the mantra "I am enough" and first formed a blade to cut away the shame, self-doubt and trauma, all of the necrotic tissue that was surely killing him and then formed a bandage to wrap around all the exposed flesh. This book is the surgeon's manual for that process.

"Loving yourself is not ego
It's a means of survival
In a world that insists
You are not lovable."

Through this collection of poems, notes to self, diary entries, and short personal essays, the reader tracks one femme man's journey towards forgiveness of others and forgiveness of self.

What it means to love oneself, Rivera simply and eloquently explains, is not self-obsession or self-aggrandizement but the generous extension of permission to exist as we are. We are a grievously stunning collection of joy, pain, beauty and ugliness. Instead of giving someone else the power to curate our lives, we must be courageous enough and fierce enough to handle ourselves with care: to prune what needs to be pruned and water what needs be watered. Rivera does not present a strictly chronological narrative of his healing process because healing isn't linear. He wavers back and forth, waltzing with his grief, knowing that one day he will give up the dance entirely.

Quoting Susan Sontag, a friend once mentioned that solitude is the state of "being together with oneself". This book is a journey from loneliness to solitude. Sometimes we just need to know that someone has haunted the same lonely aisles and has found their true self among the shelves and dingy corners. There is good work to be done when we take the time to be alone with ourselves. Rivera undertakes that work with readiness and with grace.

"During our last session together, Daisy gave me a glass owl that was given to her by her first therapist. That owl is perched on my desk at work and serves as a constant reminder that I've begun the process of healing." May Drafts be your glass owl, a clear cutting vision of healing in the darkness. May it be more than a book. May it be a beacon.

Read *Drafts* because it is deeply intimate and courageous. Not enough stories like Rivera's exist in the light.

Age: 14

I was discovering the joys
Of kissing other boys
Puberty began to change the parts of me
I pretended didn't exist
I was a blooming faggot.

Marking My Own Path: An Inner City Dreamer

Langston Hughes once asked, "What happens to a dream deferred?"

Looking back at my childhood, here's my answer: the dream deferred sits idle like a neighborhood grandmother. She waits on the porch to greet children returning home from school.

It is a dandelion trying to make its way through the crack in the concrete, straining to bloom. It bounces off walls like stray bullets that threatened a child's life, long before he could even form a dream. It becomes the first full night's sleep for the newborn baby so its teenage mother doesn't have to lose all hope. It becomes the rage of a people who still believe in Dr. King's dream, but know it has yet to be fully realized.

For many young boys of color who grow up in inner cities, the "hood," "ghetto," or the "slums," sometimes it's hard to see beyond the city limits and to believe in the power of dreams.

I am a Latino, raised in a single-mother household, living below the poverty threshold, a product of the public school system, a statistic we often hear about those who look like me. Regardless of the systematic oppression I have endured, I never lost hope. I knew from an early age that I would have to mark my own path—that if I wanted to pursue my dreams, I would have to do it on my own.

However, it wasn't until the death of my brother that I realized that life was too precious to let fear stop me from living as my authentic self. I was 14 years old when my older brother, Kamal, was killed at the age of 22. For about a year, I stopped writing. I stopped caring about school. I was overwhelmed by grief. I decided that I needed to live openly as a gay man. I was afraid of backlash I would get from family and friends but I knew that I did not want to waste time lying. The decision to "come out," or as writer and scholar Darnell L. Moore puts it, "invite in," was an act of liberation for me.

Coming out and expressing my gender in a way that does not conform to social norms allowed me to live the life I was created for—as an artist and activist.

I am 23 years old, and am the first person in my immediate family to graduate from high school. And from college. I understood that education was going to be the key to breaking the cycle of dreams deferred. Obviously, navigating higher education, as a first generation college student, was not easy. I was fortunate to have people in my life that believed in my dreams and in me. They say it takes a village to raise a child. I believe the same holds true for dreams. It takes a village to nurture the dreamers and their dreams. Now I live my dreams out loud. I travel the country and speak about lesbian, gay, bisexual, transgender, and queer (LGBTQ) issues, disability and dance, and share my writing with the world.

As a kid growing up with cerebral palsy, I found comfort in writing in my journal. Being forced to sit on the sidelines as the other kids played left me yearning to belong to a different world. Writing was my escape. Since the third grade I have been writing poetry and always knew I wanted to grow up to be a storyteller.

For a long time I struggled with guilt because I was trying to understand why I was able to make it out alive, while others in Paterson, New Jersey, found themselves in the crossfire of bullets or victims of hate crimes because of their sexuality and gender identity. Yet I had the privilege of going to college and of speaking at New York University, Harvard University and other institutions of higher learning and sharing my story.

Today I am dedicated to helping others like me, youth of color from inner cities, LGBTQ youth, people with disabilities, and first generation college students. I want to inspire them to form their own path, to take the road less traveled, and to break the generational cycles of dreams deferred in their own lives. I am one inner city dreamer of the countless thousands of youth that imagine that there's more to life than what they see around them or in the media. Marking my own path was not just something I did for myself. I wanted to show folks what is possible when they refuse to give up on their dreams.

In the words of John Lennon, "You may say I'm a dreamer but I'm not the only one."

In the Distance: In Memory Of...

I will always hold you near
No matter how far away
Through the pain and the tears
Our memories will never go astray
It's the distance one fears
Knowing you're so far away
In the distance I'll see your face
And that glowing light of grace
Just knowing you're in a better place
Makes the distance fade away.

To my brother Kamal, may you continue to rest in peace.

Four Who Passed Along Important Life Lessons

Many may recall their childhood teacher as an old woman who scrunched up her nose and pointed her index finger at them whenever they did something wrong, but for me that was not the case.

I always had relatively young teachers, who were modern and knew all the latest music and fashion trends; they were great teachers. The best lessons I ever learned in the classroom were not scholastic. They were life lessons taught by four teachers in particular.

During my difficult years in middle school, one teacher stood out. Her name was Madelynn Walker. My sixth-grade language arts teacher, she was the woman responsible for my love of writing and encouraged me to pursue writing seriously. She told me to believe in myself, and in my ability to write.

More importantly, she held me accountable for my actions. She never allowed her students to use their upbringing or their surroundings as an excuse not to succeed. This advice was given partly because of her own experiences. She had also grown up in Paterson, New Jersey, went on to higher education and became successful despite the obstacles. Her life lesson was to be a leader and to believe in your dreams.

Another middle school teacher who made a difference was my eighth-grade language arts teacher, Melissa Bonadies. She saw her students as her equals and never looked down on us simply because she was an adult and we were children. Not only was she great at teaching English, she was great at listening to her students when they had problems.

She always assured me that things would be better one day, and that the things that happened then wouldn't matter once I was in high school. And she was right. She reminded me that there was a bigger and better future waiting for me. All I had to do was stay focused, and I could do anything. Her life lesson was to keep on going on, because the future was filled with promise.

My high school journalism teacher, Tara Kane, quickly became my favorite. She gave all of her knowledge to her students, and although I only had the pleasure of being taught by her for two years, she planted the seed for the flower I would blossom into. She was always hard on me while in class, but I knew she just wanted me to be the best that I could be. She taught me the essentials of being a journalist and the importance of staying true to myself.

Another lesson that I learned from her was that a plan is always tentative and never concrete. She made me realize that life can change in an instant, and I should always be prepared to trash my plan and see where life takes me.

My mentor and dance teacher at school, Erin Pride, was the woman who took me under her wing and changed my life dramatically. When my passion for dance flared, she was the woman who molded me into the dancer I became because she took the time to believe in me.

She always pushed me to work hard. Her life lesson was in not the words she may have spoken to me; it was her way of teaching by example. She showed me that hard work was always worth the stress, the pressure, the sweat and tears, because the end result is always worth it.

I think most people don't realize how important teachers are in shaping who they become. I also think teachers often don't fully realize how important they are. Even years later, their lessons continue to guide students, long after those students have left their classrooms behind.

Ode to My Body

Forgive me for I have forsaken you,
Thrown you between the lion's jaw
Pushed you to the core of your being
Until you began to break

Crippled,
Frail,
Sore,
Bruised,
Stiff

Still I adore you.

We met at conception
You were premature
Given the task of being my keeper
Of holding my soul within you

Tired,
Beaten,
Swollen,
Limited,
Exhausted

Still I adore you.

For without you,
I could not be the dancer
You have given me the facility to live my dreams
I adore you and all your glory,

No matter how worn out you are,
No matter how your stomach expands,
No matter how your muscle spasms interrupt my sleep

Remember that I adore you
Even as I run us both to the ground.

To My Father

Dear Papi,

Every Father's Day, I am sad, angry, confused, and hopeful.

As I flip through the family photo albums, I hunt for snapshots of you and me. Sadly, there aren't any to find. I am writing you because regardless of being missing in action, you are half of the reason why I am alive.

For years, I thought you left because of something I did. It took a shitload of therapy to realize it was not my fault that you were a deadbeat dad. More recently I discovered that it isn't entirely your fault either. You were simply following in the footsteps of your dad, who modeled what it meant to be an absent dad -- to leave a child behind in order to raise another family. Maybe you thought I didn't deserve to have your last name. Then, you slut shamed my mother and planted seeds of doubt that made me think it was her fault. But when you requested a DNA test, I understood I was simply the victim in a war between you and my mother.

I spent most of my childhood yearning for your presence. Wanting you to teach me how to play sports, get the ladies, and knot a tie. Instead the lessons you passed on to me were learned in the two summers I traveled to Buffalo, New York, to see you, and in the years of hoping you'd remember my birthday. It's going on 26 years and I can't remember a time when you've wished me a happy birthday.

I learned that it wasn't okay to physically and verbally abuse women. I learned that drug addiction can lead to destruction and the death of a relative. I learned that you were simply repeating a cycle. I don't think your father was the best example of a dad. I had to learn to define my own manhood. It took me years to get comfortable in my skin, to trust that I wouldn't turn out like you.

No amount of awards, accomplishments, or supportive love from my chosen family will fill the void formed by your absence. I've tried everything–lusting after men, putting myself out there on hook-up apps, and trying to affirm that I am worthy of a man's love by offering him my body. The void only grew bigger. If I am being completely honest, I am outraged.

Papi, I've spent the last few years working on myself, unpacking my shame and embracing my imperfections. I've learned how to talk about my shame and how to reach out when I feel overwhelmed by my shame gremlins.

I have come to understand that your actions and your absence have nothing to do with me.

I don't want kids, partially because I'm afraid to repeat the cycle you have mastered with all seven of yours. But if I ever change my mind, I will make sure that the children will feel my presence. I will teach them the importance of love and being people of integrity. I will give them my last name and make sure they never question their connection to me.

So, I wish you a Happy Father's Day and thank you for allowing my existence to take shape. Thanks for the lessons and for reminding me that there are many pathways to manhood and that I chose differently than you.

Your son,

Mark

Matthew's Way

There's a hint of orange in your hazel eyes
As a child, I thought those eyes would get you far in life
Women would line up; success was yours for the taking
Your dirty blond hair and caramel skin
You were a handsome boy
But somehow life did not pan out
The way your mother hoped

You fucked up
Repeated his ways
The man who never knew how to be a dad
You held onto that rage
As you entered her raw
Planting seeds you never intended to nurture
You lied, cheated, and stole
It was the only way you knew

You struggled to admit he touched you
You only knew how to repeat
The cycle, becoming a runaway criminal
On the run
On the run
On the run

But you
Can never outrun the voices in your head
From the city of sins
To the city of red socks
To eventually finding yourself
Exhausted from the run
Boxed in
Like a captive bird

The orange jumpsuit
Compliments your hazel eyes.

Moving Through Perfectionism

It's March of 2009 and I turn to my best friend Jennifer and say: "I want to start my own dance company for disabled and non-disabled dancers." I was only 17 years old when I made that proclamation and as a disabled person, my new found passion for dance would take me down an unforgettable path. My dance company, marked dance project, would open many doors of opportunity for me.

In the fall of 2013 my friend Andrea Kramer and I began discussing the possibility of having me as a guest choreographer for Ballet Forte at Wings Conservatory, a pre-professional dance school in New

Jersey. I was interested in working with BFWC and, having been a guest teacher in the past, I knew her students were hard workers and had a strong foundation of technique.

I remember feeling intimidated as I walked into the studio on audition day alongside the other guest choreographers, one a New York University graduate, the other a BFWC alum, and then there was this fierce woman who was an assistant to an established choreographer. All of them had formal dance education under their belts, including degrees in dance and choreography. Meanwhile, I was working on a degree in women's and gender studies with minors in journalism and public relations. However, like I had in much of the seven years in my dance career, I did what felt authentic to me. I did what I've become known for; I pushed the dancers to show me their artistry, and not just their technique. As a person with a disability, I can't do all the things that are typical and expected of men who dance, but being the communicator that I am, I learned how to use my body, and the bodies of my assistants, and my words to express to the dancers what I was envisioning in my head.

Initially, I had no idea what I was going to set on the six dancers that I picked from the audition, but I knew I wanted it to be reflective on the past year of my life. I was already working on a new piece for my company, "Our America," which explored the social issues around gun violence in our country, and knew that I wanted this piece to be a strong contrast to any of the group work I have ever done before. I wanted to challenge myself to go deeper, not to be afraid to push boundaries, and to remain true to the story I was trying to tell through movement.

The biggest lesson I learned was through the interactions I had with the dancers -- many of who were in their early teens. What I was asking of them took a great deal of maturity and commitment. I was trying to tell the story of my life in the past year, how I struggled with perfectionism, and did not want to show my true self. I had spent years hiding behind a mask, trying to deal with the lows and blows that came from vulnerability. "The Unmasking" represents my own journey through self-discovery and awareness. It was my daring greatly moment, the end result of the courage I had gathered to remove my own mask, to give up trying to be perfect and allow myself to be flawed, to be fully human. One of the dancers, who was also struggling with perfectionism, was overextended and the pressure to be perfect was making her world crumble. She had missed hours of rehearsals -- so many that I had to threaten to remove her from the piece if she did not fully commit to the process.

Anyone that knows me well knows that I am a big softy but I have high standards for any project that my name is attached to, and when the dancer showed up late again, I had to have a difficult conversation. It was the first time in my career that I resented the fact that I was not just a choreographer, but also an educator. It was my job to help this young dancer and do something that no one else around her seemed to be doing; I pushed her off the pedestal. Everyone in her life put her on a pedestal, without considering how the height would cause the fall to be that more detrimental. They were breeding her to live a life of perfection, something she would surely fail at accomplishing. I told her that I had to take her out of the piece, that I could not contribute to supporting the pedestal she was placed on and that I needed her to stop trying to be perfect.

She broke down. As she cried and pleaded with me to let her back into the piece, I held her. I cried with her. And I made her repeat the following sentence over and over again, "I am 16. I am human and I am not perfect." Once she gathered her breath, I asked her to teach her role to the other dancers and to remain a part of the creative process as an understudy. Some might think that decision was cruel, but I needed her to understand that life has a way of humbling us, and that if we respond with humility to our circumstances, there was the chance of redemption. She taught her section with grace and clarity, caring enough about the piece to make sure she taught her peers thoroughly. I had every dancer audition for her role with her watching, and while they were all talented, it was clear to me that she needed to play this role more than I needed her to. I asked the rest of the cast if they felt she should be given another chance since, after all, they were the ones being most affected by her missed rehearsal time. Each and every one of them said yes. I turned to her and said she was given one more chance.

When I began choreographing "The Unmasking"—the majority of the work was choreographed in two weekends, four rehearsals, totaling approximately 18 hours. During the time that I began setting the work, I was overextended. The truth is, I was traveling for work, writing papers for classes, employed at (two) part time jobs, working with my dance company, and I was also setting work as an alumni choreographer for my high school. Knowing I needed to slow down, we didn't have additional rehearsals until a month later. This is not common for me, to begin work and not fully finish it, and then to have so much time in between. But I was practicing the lesson I had been trying to teach the dancer. I told myself, "I am 22. I am human and I am not perfect."

As the dancers and I returned to the studio to finish the work and clean the piece, I saw the entire piece with a renewed perspective and began changing the choreography and the music. Two days before the premiere, we had our final cleaning rehearsal and by the end of the two hours, we had boiled down the past year of my life into nine minutes. On Wednesday, we premiered "The Unmasking" and the audience reactions assured me that the entire process was worth it. All of the dancers did exactly what I asked of them. They performed and spilled their souls on that stage. I lost my breath as I saw it for the first time in full costume and on stage, with the lights.

The most intimate piece I have ever choreographed, "The Unmasking" and the process to create it will always hold a special place in my heart. Taking our masks off can be difficult but not nearly as difficult as trying to be perfect. Perfectionism is something we strive for but never something we attain. Remember that you are human and innately imperfect. Put your mask down, show us your flaws and all and cry if you have to.

16 Rounds

There are only two types of killers—
Those with no authority to shoot and
Those whose badges give them authority to
Pull the trigger

One too many shots
Fired to the back
Of the head

The black boy is dead
I mean the "criminal," "thug," and "drug user"

No, I mean every black and brown boy in America
No, I mean every black and brown girl in America
Because the victim is created in the image of Goliath
While the officer, the killer
Is made to look like David

Age: 22

Love is elusive—
Your greatness they adore
Your heart they ignore.

From Behind Closed Doors

I never knew how powerful it would feel to speak—and how having someone else listen would heal my brokenness.

As a Latino, I was taught that speaking about my problems that occurred behind closed doors was not permitted. From a young age, I was taught not to trust individuals, such as therapists, because therapy was "what white people did" and "you are no gringo, you don't talk to people about what happens in this house." Suffering in isolation during my first semester in college, I was frequently crying and unable to stop.

One day I could not get out of bed. The depression came over me and I became physically ill. That day marked the darkest moment in my transition from high school to college. As I tried to reflect on the lessons taught in my freshmen seminar course, I remembered a therapist, a woman who spoke about emotional intelligence, a fellow Latino, Daisy Rodriguez. On November 21, 2010, I reached out to Daisy and began therapy. On that day, I took the first steps in the process of healing and found someone who would truly listen.

At first I never discussed going to therapy with others because I was ashamed, but in time I learned to embrace it. As an advocate for therapy, I encourage people to seek help and remind them that they are not alone. Daisy had become my sounding board, an ear for all of my concerns, and an anchor in the midst of the storm. From issues with my mother, to break-ups, school challenges, and my successes, I had Daisy to share it all with. She was there for me every step of the way; with her objectivity, her affirming nods, and her sincere concern for my well-being.

Daisy is a tiny woman with ginger curls, who often blends into the background of a room. Her soft-spoken voice saved me from the pit of my depression; she got me through my suicidal ideations, and got me through a dark period when my life flashed before my eyes. Daisy is my hero—she has an "E" on her chest because her empathy, ability to encourage me, and our shared experiences have kept me from dealing with my demons alone.

During the low points, I found solace knowing that I had Daisy to help me. I was able to speak knowing that she listened to every single word, analyzed every story and my body language, and then asked me a profound question or two, which always challenged me to reflect and come to realizations I kept trying to ignore.

After graduation, my time with Daisy came to an end. It felt worse than a break-up; I was losing someone I had learned to trust with all my secrets. During our last session together, Daisy gave me a glass owl that was given to her by her first therapist. That owl is perched on my desk at work and serves as a constant reminder that I've begun the process of healing.

From behind the tightly shut doors of my childhood and teenage years, I reached out to a woman who deemed me worthy of helping—by answering my email, she began my journey towards healing; she became my healer.

On Loving Men Beyond the Erection

My sexuality is not about sex.

Regardless of what the media, the church, or politicians say, my sexuality is not defined by my sexual behaviors or by the size of my penis. I am attracted to men. I admire men. My desire for other men doesn't stem from an erection but from the intimacy I have with men that I can't have with women.

For men reading this who also enjoy loving other men, you probably can relate to the experience of coming to grips with the attraction you felt for the same gender. I was 12 the first time I kissed another boy; I was 14 when I came to the realization that the feelings I felt toward boys were not accidental or experimental.

Our society is saturated with the idea that sex sells. Patriarchy has conditioned us to view women simply as bodies and gay men as defective members of manhood. For a long time I struggled to separate the act of sex from my sexuality. I thought being gay meant being a top, the person who penetrates, or a bottom, the one who is penetrated, and being fearful of vaginas.

It was only when I began my LGBTQ activism work that I realized that being gay meant so much more to me than just whom I slept with or what body part a man has. For me, being gay means daring to be revolutionary by loving another man no matter what society thinks or says about it.

One day I met a man who turned my world upside down and helped me redefine what my sexuality means to me. This guy, whom I will refer to as "James," was attractive. He had this way with words, and a smile that took my breath away. James happened to be transgender and was assigned "female" at birth.

The first time I met James, I was walking down a hallway at the Northeast LGBTQ Leadership Conference in Rochester, NY. When he passed by me, I instantly turned around and introduced myself because I recognized him from a photo that Janet Mock, the TV host and advocate shared on her Facebook page. He smiled, and in that moment my mind was blown. James had me captivated. He did not have to worry about disclosure with me, because I had already heard about his work as a trans advocate. The attraction was overwhelming, and I found myself conflicted. "How could I be attracted to him? What does this mean about my gayness?"

Over a period of several months, I fell for James. I remember our first kiss; it took place outside under the bright lights of abandoned downtown Brooklyn in the middle of the night. Few people were around, and I felt like I was in a movie. I remember when James surprised me and flew out to Miami, where I was vacationing. We spent two nights jamming to Beyoncé, watching movies, and cuddling. I came to understand that my ability to love men was not restricted to their erections; that my ability to love men was not determined by genitalia. I discovered this in part because of James.

For me, intimacy isn't found in a penis but in the way my lover's hands melt into mine. The way he stares into my brown eyes and lets me know that he is looking into my soul and isn't afraid of my darkness. The way he assures me that I am enough. It's the swagger in his walk, the way he talks. Intimacy, for me, is beyond penetration. It is the ability to sleep beside another man, to touch, to hold and affirm without having to penetrate. For me intimacy is being able to cry in front of him, go without make-up and leave my hair messy.

I am calling on all my gay, bisexual, and queer cisgender men to start talking about our attraction and love for all men — including men who are of the trans experience -- because our ability to love and to be loved runs deep. Deeper than the shallowness that often surrounds our interaction with other men.

Blank

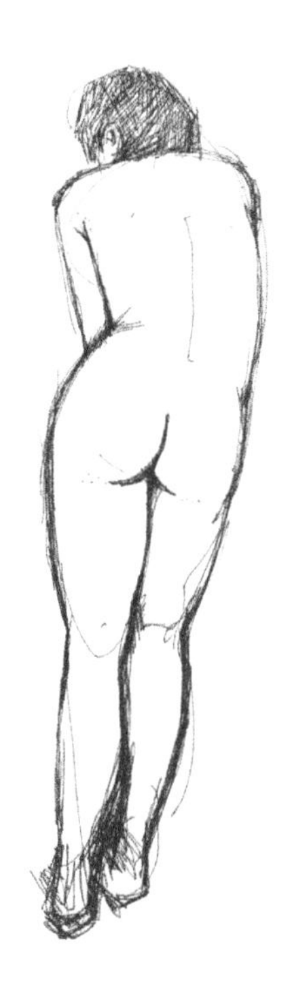

Arching my back
To snap the perfect shot
I'm bare.
Maybe this will make him react,
Make him so erect
That he won't notice how empty I am.
I'm blank
All that remains is shame.

Arching my back
He does not even know my name,

All he knows is that I'm thick,
Uncut, curvy, and unafraid to show it all.
He may think I'm easy,
Another fast track.

Arching my back
Inviting a stranger's touch,
Lusting for his lips as I sway
My hips side to side,
Waiting for a momentary rush
Between the sheets.
All that remains is a body filled with shame.

Arching my back
Snap after snap,
Pretending it was just a photo.
It did not mean anything.
He could look but not touch
Until I found myself in the back seat of his car.
I felt cheap
My lower back pressed against the door
Trying to ignore every thought telling me
"You deserve more"

Arching my back
So another stranger could hit my spot.
He said,
"You could build walls with the bodies
You've given your all.
Did any of them ever make love to you?"

Sailing Dreams

There is something to be said about a love that transcends--
Immaturity,
The transition from high school
To college,
From fantasies to realities

In the years since I first laid eyes on you,
I still catch myself in awe
I stare into your brown eyes and my sails set
Drifting from coast to coast,
From east to west
Down to the south,
To the very core of my being

This must be what love feels like at sea
The waves crashing against this ship we've created,

The wood has your name engraved in it
And the flag that I hung,
Proves that I've fought and loved hard

Now I prepare to say goodbye,
I can't ride the waves with you this time,
Your dreams are calling you out to sea,
Crossing oceans and overcoming fear
Maybe I can become a mermaid
Maybe your love for me can transform me
Once more, like it has done over and over again
Our dreams are sailing to different seas
But I'll meet you at the dock,
Waiting for you to come home,
With a dream realized,

And when I feel as blue as the bottom of the sea,
I will remember our transcendent love.

An Open Letter to Dr. Brené Brown

Dear Dr. Brown,

As a Latino, as a man, I have been conditioned not to talk about my problems (or my shame), and not to be vulnerable.

In your book, *Daring Greatly*, you urge your readers to own their story, so I am writing to share with you how your work has been helping me cope with my shame.

Recently, I was diagnosed with depression. The shame that has been building for several months reached a new high — my diagnosis was just another statistic to add to my list. As if being Latino, gay, disabled, and poor wasn't already enough, I was now adding depression to my life's roster of marginalized identities. The shame I felt in that moment was two-fold.

First, I was ashamed of who I was, of this new me that now also included mental illness. Then, I felt shame in how I believed others would now think of me.

In the summer of 2013, I was living in California and completing an apprenticeship. For the first time in my adult life, I had moved far away from my support system. I grew up in New Jersey; I am an East Coaster through and through, but my experience traveling from east to west would impact my life in a way I could not imagine.

It was during my time in California that I was able to really dig deep within myself to address the trauma of sexual abuse that helped me rise to new heights and then reach such lows — the trauma that in many ways continues to be unexpressed. I found myself drowning in shame as I continued my journey of self-awareness and discovery.

While in California, I was reunited with an ex-boyfriend. Our time together, in his hometown, was one of the most rewarding yet heartbreaking experiences I've ever had. I remember walking around Oakland and hearing stories from his childhood. I was getting insight into his life and all of the darkness that seemed to plague him. One drunken night he and I kissed and I remember hoping it would turn into something more. But it didn't and our arguments over that summer would teach me a lot about accepting the fact that he and I would never be together again. It was the experiences I had with him that made me realize I was in a lot of trouble because I had a hard time letting go. I had fallen in love with the potential of the man staring into my eyes instead of accepting the man as he stood before me. The night after we had our intimate encounter, I was sitting on my balcony looking out at Lake Merritt and drinking wine; at this point shame was just a whisper.

While living in Oakland, I saw you on *Oprah's Super Soul Sunday* and I was immediately in awe. Watching clip after clip on YouTube, then later discovering your TED talks — I began understanding shame and vulnerability in a way that I never had before.

In *Daring Greatly* you wrote, "We're afraid that our truth isn't enough — that what we have to offer isn't enough without the bells and whistles, without editing, and impressing." A few weeks after discovering your work, I found myself on the edge with myself — my "persona" went into survival mode and it spared no one from its wrath.

My mask had cracked, and rather than leaning into the discomfort, I was in the lion's den of life trying to crawl my way out of my own darkness. I was afraid those around me wouldn't be able to bear my truth; I was hurting, but from the outside looking in, my successes prevented many from seeing that hurt.

"When I loved so fiercely that rather than feeling gratitude and joy I could only prepare for loss — I controlled things. I managed situations and micro-managed the people around me. I performed until there was no energy left to feel. I made what was uncertain certain, no matter what the cost. I stayed so busy that the truth of my hurting and my fear could never catch up. I looked brave on the outside and felt scared on the inside." (*Daring Greatly*)

After the summer in California, I returned to my home in the East. I spoke at Harvard and New York universities, and several New Jersey colleges and universities. While I was encouraging folks to embrace themselves and their potential, little did they know that I was struggling to take my own advice behind closed doors.

As an activist, dancer, and writer I am no stranger to vulnerability; my art requires me to expose myself in order to create the work that I do. What I was failing to recognize was that even while being transparent for my art, I was holding back. I was stifling myself because I couldn't open up about the shame I had been feeling. That what I thought was an act of vulnerability was really just an act of deflection — I still was not ready to lean into the discomfort, I was not ready to embrace my imperfections.

I attempted to maintain the persona; I kept throwing myself into my work because that's the one area of my life that I have a lot of control over. My work has never let me down, has never rejected me, and my work has never betrayed me. Staying busy was how I avoided dealing with my shame.

For me shame is:

- Being diagnosed with depression
- Getting laid off from my day job and worrying about paying bills
- Opening up to someone only to have them reject me

- Being fatherless and searching for fatherly love in the arms of strangers
- Sexualizing myself because I think that's all I'm good for
- Drinking wine in order to numb the pain
- Cutting ties with the people that mean the most to me
- Walking around consumed with rage
- Screaming at anyone and anything
- Hurting others because I am hurting
- Looking at my body and feeling less than
- Making a noose out of a scarf to tie around my neck because I did not think I was worthy of living

I am coping with my shame and your work is helping me through this difficult period. So the next time you have to deal with a vulnerability hangover, the next time you doubt yourself, or the next time the "gremlins" give you hell, remember that your work is saving lives because in part, your book *Daring Greatly*, is saving mine.

As I cope with my shame I am learning to:

- Lean into the discomfort
- Love fiercely without thinking of all the ways rejection can hurt me
- Go with the flow in life
- Embrace the fact that I am enough
- Accept my diagnosis for what it is: a chemical imbalance
- Understand that there is power in vulnerability
- Forgive those who have contributed to my shame
- Forgive myself
- Give up my vices (alcohol)

- Manage my anger in a non-destructive way
- Love myself fully and unapologetically
- Accept that I only have one life to live and I can't give up on it
- Set boundaries for myself and make self-care a priority
- Speak about my shame to reclaim authority over my life

Writing this letter is my attempt to dare greatly, to lean into the discomfort, to share publicly for the first time my struggle with depression, and to thank you, Dr. Brown, for the work you are doing.

It is time that we silence the voices in our heads that tell us we are not good enough, and it is time we start shouting the phrase: "I am enough."

Best wishes,

Mark

To Slow Dance

There I lay, between all the words that were said
My sheets felt like armor,
Turning away from you
I simply laid on my side, trying to hide the tears that
Began to fall
I wanted to give you my all

But like our past, we're running on expired time
Now I'm trying to breathe again,
Still weeping in my bed
You looked down on me and said
"Stand up Mark, there's only a minute left in this song"
Knowing I was in a race with time,
Knowing I would lose again this time,
I stood up, afraid to stare you in the eyes
And you pulled me close to your chest

We began to slow dance,
Swaying side to side, turning around
We slow danced
As your embrace held me tight
It was another beautiful night
As I slow danced with a lover I can never have again

I wonder where the humor resides
How the universe could bring you back into my life
Knowing that time would only repeat
Twenty-four hours in a day,
Sweet words and the ending would remain the same

Watching you disappear into the darkness,
Passing parked cars,
My light was still on,
Hoping it would be a sign
Informing you that we can still slow dance,
That we can still share in the night
Because what kind of heart doesn't look back?

Vacancy

There's a pill in my mouth
The kind they warn you not to swallow
A void
Somewhere along the way
I lost a piece of me

Though I've been searching
Trying to fill this vacancy
I can't seem to erase my memories
Or the prints from the hands that
Have touched my body bare
I can't remove the smell of sex
From my nostrils
Unable to cleanse my soul
Rid myself of such vacancy

Maybe if I didn't give it up
Didn't allow that first touch
First erection
First sensation of ejaculation

But now that has come and gone
A battered soul
A numb mind
The vacancy expands
Until I have nothing left
No emotion
No self-love
No remorse
Just a human body
That has become vacant and hollow.

Between Two Wonders

I woke up with roses blooming in my stomach. This must be a dream, I thought, looking left and seeing the wonder that was this man, stretched out beside me. To my right the view from his eighth-story balcony shimmered like glitter. Miami's tropical weather always left me wanting more sun and less snow. I had a smile imprinted on my face like a clown's- slightly unbearable, slightly frightening, and yet freakishly understandable.

The ocean was massive and endless, as wide as the horizon and as deep as the galaxy. The sun rested its rays upon the waves as if trying to soften the blow of tides hitting the sandy shore. In the early hours of that Friday morning, the waves were small and serene, and for a moment all I could hear was the soft clash against the shore and the sound of a man breathing calmly in his sleep. I was between two wonders and both left me equally breathless. I tried to pinch myself, with weightless fingers, back to reality. This is a dream, I kept telling myself.

His existence seemed magical. He couldn't have flown so far, rented a car, and booked a hotel just to spend two nights in Miami with me. Could he? A couple of nights before, he and I had been texting. I told him I was going to write a poem about him but my ego would not let me write it. He replied, "I was going to book a ticket to Miami but my ego wouldn't let me do it." I thought he was kidding. He lived in New York City; a forty-minute train ride away from where I lived in New Jersey. Why the hell would he spend all that money just to fly down to Miami? Then he asked for my address. I started reciting my home address before realizing he was asking me for the location of my hotel in Miami. I was shocked. I did not believe that a guy would go out of his way to make me feel special. Shortly after he sent me a photo of his hotel room. He was already there.

I have always been the guy that other guys run away from. I was not the guy who ever was told that I was worthy, or loved, or special. I looked at his selfie and instantly blushed. I could not stop smiling; I could not stop laughing; this was unreal. It did not feel real until he picked me up in his rental car and started driving me to his hotel room. As I stared out the window at the high rises and nightclubs, and parked cars as he zipped by, all I could think about was the night he and I spent together two months before.

It had been a disaster. My feelings for him were growing stronger but he had a way of leaving me feeling insecure and uncertain. I was always pondering whether or not I was in this alone, whether I was the only one that cared deeply, if I was the only one falling in love. Earlier that day we had spent some time cuddling but when it came time to go to sleep, he did not suggest that I lay beside him but instead slept in the spare bed in my dorm room. I desperately wanted to lie beside him. In the middle of the night I crept over and lay next to him. I asked if I could hold him. Half asleep, he said yes. But what he really wanted to say was no, as I would later learn in one of our arguments. What he really wanted was for me to stay in my own bed. He felt violated, despite the fact that he asked me to rub on his chest, despite the fact that he grabbed hold of my penis until I climaxed.

We were navigating the grey space between the black and white of our lives; his brown skin against my lighter skin. We were both unsure about what it all meant. All he knew was that I was falling for him and all I knew was that I was the one who would have a lot to lose. Men threw themselves at him left and right. He was the popular kid and I resorted back to my middle school self: the awkward kid who was not liked, never popular, and definitely not desired.

After an encounter, we'd go weeks without talking. Finally, after several intense conversations we decided that we both cared for one another. A few days later he arrived in Miami. As we drove to his hotel I did my best to create small talk because I did not just want to keep staring at him. He kept asking what I was looking at but I just could not believe that he was within reach. As we approached the hotel and entered the room I was relieved to see two full-size beds. Why?

The truth was that I have been damaged by past trauma. Shortly before he arrived in Miami, I had decided to share with my godmother that I had been abused as a child by both boys and girls in my family. I had been suppressing the memories because one abuser was someone in my immediate family and I could not handle remembering how that person had treated me. As a young gay man, society had conditioned me to believe that my only value was my body and the sexual behaviors I would participate in. I realized that in my attempt to ignore the deeply rooted shame, in my attempt to pretend that none of it happened, I was repeating the cycle of abuse. The truth was, I struggled with intimacy; I struggled to accept the fact that a guy could hold me without having to fuck me.

There he lay with his eyes shut, at peace, laying in the glow of his wonder. I woke up to him on my left—a man who had to design his own path. There, with his black tank top and his grey underwear, lay a man who I had come to care for deeply. The wrinkles around his eyes, the lines on his forehead—proof of his struggle, proof of his laugher, proof that he has lived a life that at times aged him far too fast. Maybe it was the effect of the testosterone shots, but it did not matter because as he smiled and said, "I know I'm cute in my sleep." He must have felt the heaviness of my awe stricken gaze. I rolled my eyes and silently agreed with him. I did not want him to think I thought he was as beautiful, as handsome, as wonderful in my eyes as the ocean was in the eyes of the countless that sought it out daily.

I did not want to be one who fell off a cliff, feeling my body crash into the ocean's thin but powerful armor. I did not want to be the one who fell for a man who would put in the effort to make me feel this special. I didn't want to get caught in the in-between again, lost in translation, trying to determine what it all meant to have him in bed next to me. All I could think about was the tragic ending that was surely coming. Shame, fear, and experience taught me that anticipating rejection would lessen the hurt of being walked out on, of having someone decide that despite how great he thought I was, I was not worth stepping into the arena for.

What I did not know was that the two nights I spent with him in Miami would be our last. It would be the last time he wrapped his arms around me, the last time I'd lay my head against his chest, the last time our lips would meet, the last time we'd stare into each other's eyes. Weeks after our return from Miami, we argued. I was tired of existing in limbo: we were "just friends"—but we were friends who kissed one another. We were friends who shared intense intimate moments. We had romantic experiences when we hung out but they were never on a "date." I was in need of certainty and he was persistent in not wanting to provide it.

Between two wonders exists one definite truth: love is not always shared in an equitable manner. My love for him could not knock down his walls; it could not make him take all of my love with him. Instead of embracing all of me, he pushed me over the cliff. He let me fall with no intention of catching me before I hit the hard sand. I think of him daily. I think about our final nights together and sometimes it hurts my heart to carry the love I still have for my dream man. It hurts to know that he walked away, proving to me once more that love is elusive. It is my greatness they adore but my heart they ignore, that despite how wonderful they claim I am, there's something about me that prevents them from fully loving me. Between two wonders I am forced to face my worn out, bitter, hurt, scared, and lonely self. I am forced to remind myself that I am enough, that I am indeed deserving of love and belonging.

Cover Me

Cover me I am nude
Exposed
Bare to the bone
Isolated and alone

Cover me like make-up
Masking imperfections on this face
Creating an illusion of grace

Cover me
Be the shirt on my back,
Shoes on my feet
Dig deep
To cover and discover me.

Age: 24

Loving yourself is not ego
It's a means of survival
In a world that insists
You are not lovable.

Coping With Depression

Some days I force myself to sleep so I don't have to feel the emotions rushing through me. Some days I drink too much. Some days I stuff my mouth until my cheeks are sore from chewing. Some days I start to cry and have no idea why.

When I was diagnosed with clinical depression a few years ago, I was not surprised. As a Puerto Rican, I am aware of that there are higher rates of depression in the Puerto Rican community than in the

United States. The Albert Einstein College of Medicine of Yeshiva University and the Hispanic Community Health Study/Study of Latinos found that, "First-and second-generation Hispanics/Latinos were significantly more likely to have symptoms of depression than those born outside the U.S. mainland." According to the study, despite the higher likelihood of symptoms, Puerto Ricans are less likely to use antidepressants. When you take my ethnicity and sexual orientation into account, I belong to two marginalized groups that are underrepresented and under researched in the mental health profession. Too often *mi gente* have relied on the Church to help us heal, but prayer alone isn't enough to mend the brokenness.

I grew up in a household where we never discussed our problems. When my ex-stepdad turned our living room into a junkyard whenever he got angry and started breaking things, we simply cleaned up and pretended it hadn't happened. We never discussed it; instead we normalized the situation as if somehow adopting the new normal would make the experience less traumatic. Our silence about our pain and trauma keeps us imprisoned and, quite frankly, I am tired of feeling like a prisoner in my own life.

If I want freedom then I have to heal the broken little boy within me who struggles with the fact that he was molested by multiple relatives. My use of sex to numb is just my way of trying to take ownership of my own body. But I know that isn't healthy or productive—I am more than my body.

If I want freedom, then I have to heal the broken little boy within me who struggles with being abandonment by his father. I'm tired of trying to fill the void that my dad created and I know I need to forgive him for not knowing how to be a parent to me.

Coping with my depression for me means using antidepressants, talk therapy, and cultivating a strong support system. Maybe you don't have access to medicine or therapy or even a strong support system but I urge you to remember that you are not alone. It is easy to allow depression to control our thoughts, often dark thoughts that make us feel less than or unworthy of being alive.

But you and I are worthy of being here, alive.

Paperback

Some of us don't have the privilege of being stealth
To be stacked on the shelf
Of blending in with every hardcover
Sometimes we are paperback
The kind that bends but refuses to break
Proclaiming a big "fuck you" to your binary
To the check in and out process
Because our stories still have value
Our lives still matter
So stare at us
Make your snarky remarks
Tell us how we're to blame because we refuse
To be the same
To conform
To be put on a shelf, imprisoned

By your ideals of normativity
We won't apologize for being seen
For allowing our cover to reflect
All of our fierce, femme, gay colors
We'll keep bending gender
Like a paperback's spine that refuses to break.

Why Our Need for Closure Makes Us Selfish

How many times has a relationship ended and you felt as if something was left unfinished because you did not get the closure you wanted?

I had an epiphany when my best friend from college, Shaneyce called me on the phone for one of our routine chats, and checked me for nagging about wanting closure.

"You aren't going to get closure. You need to move on without it!" she said.

"But the least he could do for me is give me an explanation as to why things ended," I said.

"You're being selfish. You're asking someone to do something they may not feel ready, if ever, to do," she insisted.

If you are like me, you have experienced this on a few different occasions and it never gets easier to cope with. How do we begin to move on without closure and why should we?

The answer is simple yet difficult to practice: we have to move on because lingering in the past prevents us from living in the now and embracing future prospects for love. Closure is a selfish desire and not something we actually need in order to begin our healing process. We must remember to separate our needs from our wants: we can live without our wants but our life requires that our most basic needs be met at all times.

Reasons Our Need for Closure Is Selfish:

> *We are the ones who want closure and it does nothing for the other people we have been in a relationship with.*

Most likely they have already moved on. Especially if they were the ones to decide that things needed to end. Although they decided to separate, our "need" for a proper ending is preventing them from making a clean break.

We are demanding that someone does something they don't want to do.

The other person is not obligated to give us closure. The closure is for us and we must take the first step in moving on, and closure will surely follow.

We are trying to reclaim power we never lost.

Every time we fiercely hold onto our want for closure for the sake of regaining power, we must remember that we never lost power. We gave someone else power over us and in that process we stopped using our own power. There's no need to reclaim our power, we just need to tap into it again. We can reconnect with our power by letting go of the fantasy of closure and accept the reality of the situation: the relationship is over.

The ending of any kind of relationship can be difficult but I am a firm believer that every season ends so that something more beautiful can bloom. View every ending as an opportunity to start over, renewed, with a clean slate.

The next time you let your desire for closure prevent you from doing what's best for you, remember that you are the only one left to suffer. Don't forget that vulnerability isn't a sign of weakness, but instead a sign of strength. Move on and if the other person decides to give you closure, please know that the other person is being selfless — but you should never expect that everyone will be as selfless as them.

Product

Everyone has their insecurities
Everyone has their fears,
Everyone has shed their fair share of tears
Everyone has malfunctioned.

I, like everyone, am flawed
I, an imperfect creation.
Like a glass with a crack in it,
Like a jewel without its shine
I am a malfunctioning product.

Yet, even with imperfections
I try to present myself as a product worth obtaining,
But like any malfunctioning item,

I am inspected and returned to the pile,
Where others lay in filth,
In dismay because they will never be cherished.
I am just one more product, among the many
Broken, disheartened and lonely.

On Loving Myself Beyond the Imperfections

"...I am learning that the more I love myself, the less desperate I become. The inner voice I hear when I am alone tells me I am worth loving. No longer will I drown that inner voice with music, alcohol, or semen...I am having that longed-for love affair with myself at last..."

- Jalal, in the essay "Looking for Love"
from *Fighting Words: Personal Essays by Black Gay Men*

What if loving him was simply my way of avoiding having to love myself?

It was October of 2013, and I was in Boston, preparing to speak to a group of lesbian, gay, bisexual, transgender, and queer students of color for the Hispanic-Black Gay Coalition's Youth Empowerment Conference, hosted by Harvard University.

I was dually excited: it was the first time I had visited Boston and my first time speaking at an Ivy League university. This was also the first time I presented my workshop, "Embracing Yourself, Embracing Your Potential," a defining moment in my career as an activist and speaker.

During the workshop, I said:

> *It's easier to love someone else because we don't know all of their darkness. But we know ourselves too well. We know the dark secrets that we suppress. We know what we hide and sometimes what we hide is hard to love and embrace and that's why it's easier to love someone else. So we must learn to embrace our imperfections and every aspect of who we are. Now embracing something doesn't mean you have to like it, but embrace the fact that you've lived it, that you've made mistakes and you've learned from them, that you've changed and you've moved on.*

You know the cliché, "easier said than done"? If I'm being completely honest, it applies here. I was confidently speaking in front of various audiences, suggesting that they learn to embrace themselves so they could embrace their potential. I was doing that—I was embracing the parts of myself that were easiest for me to manage -- my professional self. My work as an activist, choreographer, speaker, and writer always allowed me to avoid my personal shortcomings. I was still single and feeling extremely lonely; my work gave me the distraction I needed. In many ways, I found comfort in the work because it's an area I have a lot of control over.

On a personal level, I was struggling to embrace my imperfections and even worse, I was struggling to accept the failures of past relationships. After James and I stopped dating, I found myself spending more time with my first love and one of my best friends, Adam. Despite the fact that Adam and I had moved on to date other people, we never fully cut each other out of our lives. We kept insisting that we could just be friends. When it came to my career, he was one of my greatest supporters. However, I would soon come to realize that he and I were never going to be able to just be friends.

Recently I had to accept a difficult reality: the friendship with Adam was doing me more harm than good. Over six years, Adam and I would break up then make up. No matter how hard we both tried to cut one another from our lives, our connection proved to be impossible to break. I am assuming it has been so difficult for us because our connection is not one tainted with malicious intent. While it has not been perfect, it isn't the kind of connection that folks warn you to walk away from. We are not abusive to one another. He still manages to make me laugh. I still manage to make him smile, even if I annoy him. So what's the harm in all of that?

When circumstances and dreams force two people to be miles away from each other, in order for the connection to last, both people must be willing to invest in the process. However, Adam struggles to be vulnerable. Perhaps there's a part of him that thinks he can let our connection fall to the wayside because I have proven time and time again that I will be there for him no matter what. Like the time he got into a fight with a friend and needed someone to vent to, or when he thought he might have been exposed to HIV. I thought he was my forever man. His inability to step into the arena with me made me feel like it was my fault. That despite how much we care for each other, I was not enough. My love was not enough for him to show up and fully be seen. Shame coated every thought and Adam's actions, such as telling me that my weight gain was the biggest obstacle between us, made me feel unworthy. This is why our friendship was harmful to me—I had to accept that once again I shared a passionate connection with another man, and no matter how amazing these men thought I was, they were unwilling and unable to show up and be fully seen.

It was 3:22 a.m. and I had just finished reading Jennifer Lopez's book, *True Love*. As soon as I read the final sentence, I knew what I had to do—I needed to accept a difficult reality: my friendship with Adam was causing me to hate myself and I couldn't shake the feeling that I would never be good enough for him. While reading, I realized that while I was constantly doing the work on myself, I still struggled to love myself. The truth is that I was so focused on loving James and then on loving Adam again that I was not focusing on loving myself.

When it came to love, I sucked at sticking up for myself. In trying to make it work, I was settling for being treated in ways that did not reflect my true worth. And I treated myself that way, too. I was not setting the standard for how I should be loved. There was still the little boy in me who believed he didn't deserve love from another man because his own father never showed him love. I was not remaining true to myself. I was so afraid of losing my connection with

Adam that I never stopped to think: "Is this a connection that I need to disconnect from?"

During a time when a lot more of my friends are getting into relationships, engaged, married, and expecting their own children, I am getting back to loving myself. No matter how much my weight fluctuates, or how much time passes since I've gone on an actual date, or how much I struggle to embrace my imperfections, beyond all of those things, there's one truth I am learning to accept: I am worthy and deserving. I am learning to love myself wholeheartedly.

#HisNameIsBlake

Your victory generated headlines
but your loss has generated less
ink, less outcry, less backlash.
You're just another black guy,
another trans life,
lost in the pile of news
not worthy of the same attention
white trans lives generate
as if your life was less worthy than Leelah Alcorn's.
I wonder if your name was Tyler,
would it make them pay attention
would they form foundations
would they stop and listen?

Blake, I will always know and
speak your name.
it was Blake Brockington
it is Blake Brockington
it will always be Blake Brockington.
it shall not be erased from our history
your story will not get lost in misgendered translation.
I will not let them add to the isolation you endured in life.
his name was Blake
Blake Brockington.
Blake Brockington, a king.

To Be an Advocate, Inspirational, and Suicidal

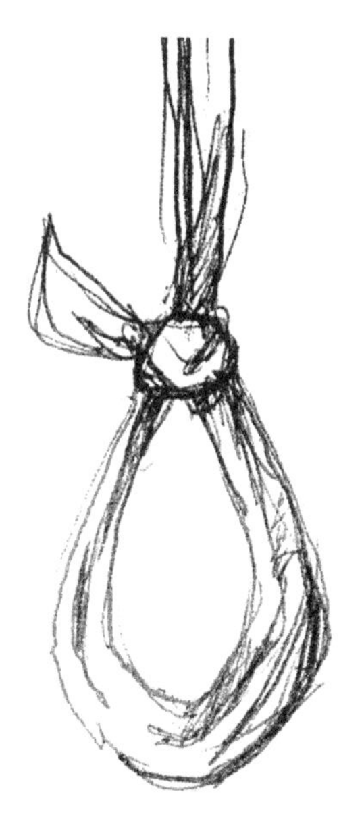

Dear Blake Brockington,

I am sorry people mistook your role as an advocate for some kind of indestructible superhero.

Too often our culture conditions us to remain silent—we have become too comfortable pleading the fifth, keeping our dirty laundry hidden, and relying on an ideology that often inflicts emotional trauma on us.

Instead of cultivating a community that allows us to talk about our issues, sadness, and shame, we are forced to endure in a silence that has resorted in the loss of too many Black and Brown lesbian, gay, bisexual, and transgender youth. It is no wonder why Black and Brown LGBT youth are two times more likely to attempt suicide than our white LGBT counterparts, according to The Trevor Project.

While you and I will never have an opportunity to meet in this lifetime, I wanted to thank you for shining your light and being brave. When I first heard you were crowned homecoming king at your North Carolina high school, becoming the first guy of the trans experience to receive the crown in your state, I was shocked and excited for you. However, I feared that the backlash might be too much of a burden. I was afraid that the pressure of the national spotlight would leave you craving for a way out, to be free.

Like you Blake, I feel the pressure that comes from being an advocate for our community. As a Latino who is gay and gender non-conforming, and who travels the country giving keynote talks, workshops, and training sessions, many have told me that I inspire them. While some may think of that as a compliment, I cannot help but feel the weight of those words. I often think, "Would they still find me so inspirational if they knew how much I cried last night? Or how difficult it was to get out of bed today? Or how I often drink to numb the pain?"

People often mistake visibility and outspokenness with strength. They assume that our willingness to speak out and help others means we no longer need help ourselves.

You once wrote on Tumblr:

> *"...I remember concluding that I'd never be enough to confront attraction. I remember realizing that there was no place for me here. I remember finding myself and finally loving him. I remember it being too late."*

I wish our paths could have crossed. I wish I could have talked to you about how this newfound attention could make it more difficult, but that you were not alone. While I was not thrown into the national headlines, I know what it means to be a winner in the midst of feeling like a loser. I know what it means to want to be free from all the voices around me that told me I was a freak, a crippled, a wannabe woman, a fag, and an abomination.

Your death has given me the courage to share this story for the first time publicly. In November of 2013 I was given an award for my contribution as an advocate to the LGBT community. It was called the Resiliency Award for Creativity, and I was truly honored to have been the inaugural recipient. About a month after receiving the award, I found myself overwhelmed with sadness. I did not want to live anymore, and the suicidal ideation I had struggled with since middle school, left me feeling hopeless. I, too, wanted to be free.

After rehearsal one Sunday evening, I made a noose out of a scarf. As I put the scarf around my neck, I thought about my family and what my death would do to them. In particular, I thought about my niece Jailyn and what she would think of me if I went through with it. That night I called the suicide hotline for the first time. Realizing that while I was great at helping others, I was not always good at helping myself. That night I realized how depression and the pressure of being an inspirational advocate almost led to an irreversible decision.

While your death did not generate as many headlines as your homecoming king victory, or as much attention as the struggles of white transgender youth, I wanted to write you this letter. I wanted you to know that I will always know your name.

Thank you for reminding me that my silence will not protect me.

In solidarity always,

Mark

12 Steps From Self-Destruction to Self-Love

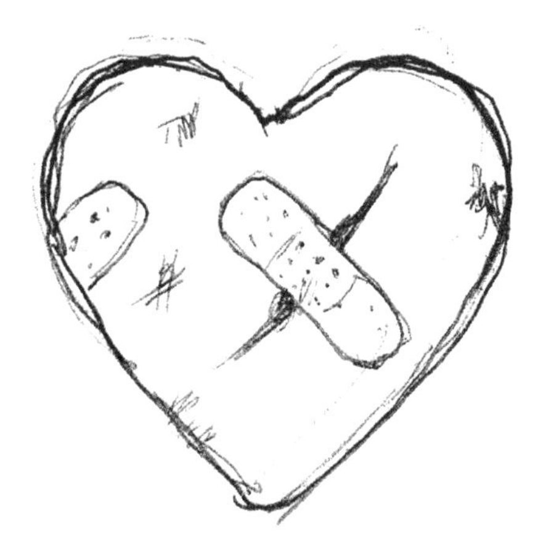

Shame is a drug without a high.

Society makes shame so easily available that we've become saturated with it and addicted to numbing it. Our media, churches, schools, governments, and families assault us with messages that insist that we are not worthy of equality, justice, or love. We are not good enough. We are imperfect.

Not skinny enough?

Not pretty enough?

Not smart enough?

Not talented enough?

Not (insert any message that society tries to trick you into believing) enough?

It's easy to collapse under the weight of shame; it's even easier to give into its allure—the belief that we will never be good enough or worthy of love and belonging. Once we accept that shame is inevitable, instead of working through it, we turn to drugs, alcohol, sex, food, and even social media to numb ourselves.

None of us are immune. In my own attempts to anesthetize, I became reckless. Drinking enough to black out, hooking up with strangers, and overeating until my stomach hurt. Even worse, I started hurting the people I loved. I jeopardized both professional and personal relationships because, in the midst of my shame storm, all I wanted to do was feel nothing. All I wanted to do was run away from the discomfort I was feeling while projecting my shame onto those who simply loved and cared about my well-being.

Many people may look at my life and assume that I have it all together. In fact, as a gay, disabled, and gender nonconforming Latino, I know that I am extremely fortunate and privileged to have a career, education, and opportunities that are often denied to others like me. Even with my accomplishments, the allure of shame and numbing continues to be a struggle. I am constantly in the process of recovery and, while I may relapse from time to time and resume self-destructive behaviors, I am committed to returning to self-love.

Just like any addiction, there's a recovery process that can take us from self-destruction to self-love, here are 12 steps to consider:

Admit that you are numbing and that shame has become unmanageable.

It took me many months, but I was finally able to admit that the shame I felt was crushing me and that, in turn, I was trying to smother it, numb it, with self-destructive behaviors. My numbing habits include having reckless sex with strangers, emotional eating, and drinking an entire bottle of white wine.

Allow your faith and love to restore you.

Whether you refer to the higher power as God or the Universe, I believe it's important to have something to believe in. My experience with the Christian church left me jaded and my faith took a backburner in my life due to the bigotry I experienced. I still struggle to accept people "laying hands on me" to pray for me. I eventually found my own path to spirituality and I allow it to restore me time and time again.

Make a decision to release the false truths that shame speaks.

Sometimes our mind tricks us into believing that a lie is truth. When I am feeling unworthy or not good enough, my mind speaks some awful things to me such as, "you will never be good enough to be successful, and you are an imposter." I am fortunate to have a strong support system that I can reach out to when the lies overwhelm me. I have learned that being met with empathy is critical to my wellbeing.

Look inward and exam yourself and areas that cause shame, numbing and wrong doing.

Self-awareness can be difficult to develop but I think it is the root of freedom. The more self-aware I have become, the freer I have felt. I have come to learn that just because one becomes self-aware, doesn't mean they always make better choices. The truth is that knowing better doesn't always equate to doing better. I remind myself daily to show myself grace.

Admit that you have been self-destructive and then share your wrongdoings.

I go to therapy every two weeks. I have learned that having an objective professional to talk to about my self-destructive behaviors is helpful. My therapist, Michael, helps me process the situation and explore the root of the problem. More often than not the root of the problem stems from my daddy issues. My dad abandoned me before I was even born, leaving my mother to raise me on her own.

Commit to coping with shame without numbing or projecting onto others.

This is perhaps the hardest step—one that I have yet to master. On the days when I can avoid numbing, I find talking about my shame with those I can trust helps me feel better. I have a handful of friends that I know I can call when I find myself in the middle of a major shame storm.

Acknowledge your weaknesses and imperfections.

I have to remind myself often that I am human, which makes me innately flawed. It means I have weaknesses and imperfections but that doesn't make me any less worthy of being loved, respected, and cherished.

Make amends with yourself and those you've hurt while self-destructing.

Making amends with those you have hurt is key to moving forward in your journey from self-destruction to self-love. While we can't change the past or undo our actions that caused people to get hurt, we can ask for forgiveness. It is not easy to ask for forgiveness but I believe we can't move forward unless we try. My best friend, Jennifer, is someone I have had to make amends with many times for my mistakes. Time and time again she has shown me grace and given me the opportunity to grow.

Continue to be self-aware and acknowledge when you're numbing and being self-destructive.

This might seem a bit repetitive but it's important to acknowledge that self-awareness isn't a one-time deal. In fact, we must make the decision to be self-aware daily. I have to tell myself on a regular basis that I am worthy and that I don't have to self-destruct in order to heal and rebuild. Numbing is tempting because for a temporary moment there is pure relief—when we numb we avoid feeling anything.

Practice empathy and forgiveness with yourself and others.

Forgiving yourself is essential in this step! While I find it easier to forgive others I care for, I find it extremely difficult to forgive myself for my mistakes. I have hurt a lot of people in the midst of the shame storm and forgiving myself for my mistakes is still an ongoing battle.

Commit to loving yourself each day.

Again, this is easier said than done but I am learning to love myself a bit more every day. I have a tattoo on my right shoulder that reads: "I am enough"—a permanent reminder that no matter what I am going through, I will always be enough.

Accept that you are enough, imperfect, and worthy of love and belonging.

Dr. Brené Brown, the research professor and best-selling author, has had a major impact on my life. Her books and talks have taught me the importance of realizing that no matter what the shame narrative says, you are enough and worthy of love and belonging. It is hard for me to remember that but I believe it to be true deep down.

The allure of accepting the shame-driven narrative in our heads is dangerous, powerful, and a constant temptation. We will fail from time to time because we are human. However, I believe that recovery, much like life, is about the journey of finding, loving, healing, accepting, and embracing ourselves.

Collide

From opposite sides of the spectrum
We collide like two ships at sea
Surrounded by fog
Never seeing the inevitable crash
Sparks ignite the waves
As you toss your anchor overboard
It crushes my chest
Breaking every bone of insecurity
You let yourself get lost in me
But you can never truly belong to me
Her Aphrodite tresses reminds you of whom you were
Before you crashed into me
Before our lips dared to touch
Though we are seas apart
Somehow I feel you
As the waves of reality collide onto my shore

I can't help but try to ignore
The distance
The miles
And the body of water across which
We wave our white flags.

What Loving a Married Man Taught Me

I have to point out that for years I told my friends that they deserved to be with men who would make them priorities. That they were worthy of being more than someone else's secret lover. Then I found myself falling in love with a married man. I know what you are thinking. "What a hypocrite!" And you might be right. But being the other person is more complicated, nuanced, and less fabulous than how it is portrayed on television. The truth is that I never expected to fall in love with her husband.

It was late at night and I spent most of the day traveling from New Jersey to Las Vegas. It was my first time in Vegas and I was about to take part in an intensive five-day leadership retreat that would change my life. That same night I met Tim. I looked like a hot mess—sweaty, messy hair, and in desperate need of sleep. Despite all of that, when he and I shook hands, we both felt a spark. .

Our affair was not consummated that night. In fact, it would take days of talking about our lives and experiences before either one of us would admit to an attraction. It wasn't just that Tim was married. Tim was also a trans guy who never imagined falling in love with a cisgender gay Latino. There was also a ten-year difference in our ages and 3,000 miles separating us once we said our goodbyes in Vegas.

A few nights after arriving in Vegas, Tim and I would have our first kiss. We stood under the stars and my right leg bent and the spark felt more like fireworks. He and I had gone back and forth about why we shouldn't kiss. But deep down I wanted to kiss him and I remained persistent, it was my stubborn side that reared its ugly face.

Gravity kept pulling us closer to one another until our lips met. Then he suddenly sprinted down the street like a middle schooler who had just kissed his crush. We both laughed. Soon the laughter turned into deep breaths and moans. We both knew he was married but as our time together in Vegas was nearing its end, it felt like it was now or never. The room was pitch black, Tim blended into the night as our lips kept touching. There was this intense feeling between us—a mixture of nervousness and excitement.

For the next few months we spoke daily; exchanging text messages for hours. The three-hour time difference made it harder but he and I were committed to whatever it was that we had with each other. My close friends told me to cut him loose. I tried several times to break it off but my heart and mind were at odds. Logically I could justify ending it with Tim. Emotionally I was invested.

The next time I saw him face-to-face was in Los Angeles. I was there for a work event and he decided to take a road trip to see me. My friend advised me that "it would start with concessions and end with heartbreak." But the time Tim and I spent together were some of my happiest moments of 2015. He introduced me to Jack in the Box, a burger joint— and I became obsessed. Tim couldn't believe that we didn't have Jack in the Box on the east coast. I introduced him to Indian cuisine but he wasn't a fan. We walked the streets of LA holding hands and the entire time I felt safe, excited, and cared for. He made me feel comfortable in a way that no other man had been able to. I could be physically and emotionally naked with him and he would still look at me with those eyes that made me know he thought I was special.

As much as he made me feel special, as much as we made each other laugh, the harsh reality was that Tim was torn between two people. He loved his wife, the person who stood by his side during his transition and had never stopped supporting him. Tim also loved me; the person he said helped him discover more about himself.

It was after our time in LA that I realized, as I lay in bed thinking about that future, that our love wasn't enough to make whatever we had work. I grew less patient with Tim and his aspirational talks about a future I knew we would never have. We would talk about the future but deep down I knew he wasn't ready to leave his wife. What I loved most about Tim was his caring nature but it was that caring nature that made him feel like he had an obligation to his wife. I also no longer wanted to be his version of Olivia Pope. While she's glamorous on the hit television show *Scandal*, in real life, there's nothing wonderful about being the second choice.

Loving a married man taught me that love is as fluid as our sexuality and gender. We can't control who ignites the spark in us, but we can set the standard for how we should be loved. Regardless of our marital status, love is complicated. After he told his wife that he was in love with me, I quickly replied to his text message and encouraged him to try to make his marriage work.

I was done conceding—my integrity, heart, and spirit demanded that I get back to loving myself. So I stood up from the table and walked away because Tim became complacent with serving me love on a platter of fantasy. He was not willing to face the fact that he would have to make a choice between his wife and me. I was no longer willing to ignore the fact that I was loving a married man.

I came to learn that I was worthy of someone choosing me, even if Tim couldn't.

Still Waiting in Line

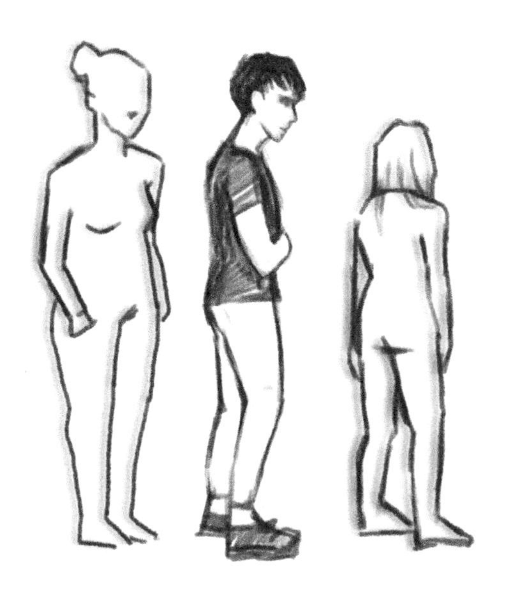

I've been standing here for quite sometime
Past the expiration date
Waiting to meet my fate
Yet, it's another hour or so
Before I am told
That waiting in line
Has been a waste of precious time

My legs ache from the strain
Of standing in this line
My heart aches from the pain
Of wondering why

Then I heard a whisper that told me to
Continue to wait
Because love knew no arrival date
And was surely worth the wait.

Crumbs

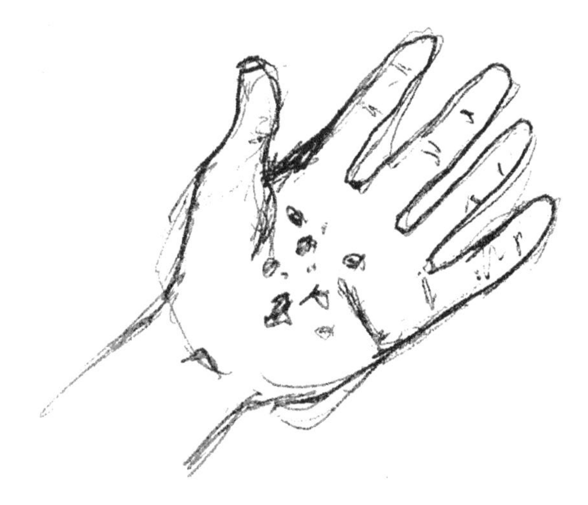

I have been operating from a space of hunger. So hungry in fact that I've been accepting mere crumbs as a whole meal. Feasting on the potential of the crumbs fulfilling me in ways they were never intended to.

I'm tired of feeling hungry all of the time. Hungry for love, joy, and meaningful connections and accepting versions of these things that aren't intended to sustain me. Some people will drop crumbs on the ground just to be able to keep you around.

The truth is that they don't care enough about you to provide you with what you are hungriest for. They half ass love you. They half ass pretend to care. They half ass believe in you. There comes a point when you get tired of half-ass people and half-ass meals.

For too long I made entrees out of crumbs. I swallowed every crumb alongside my dignity, pride, and self-respect. Ya'll I begged, cried, and yelled with my arms stretched out before me, with my palms up, waiting to see if he would provide me with the sustenance I needed. He handed me a crumb and told me to be grateful. Whenever I dared to want more, whenever I got too needy, he'd pull his hand away. It was intended to keep me in line. I had given him more power than he was worthy of having. I allowed him to deprive me of my most basic needs all in the name of love.

I am worthy of a whole fucking meal. I am worthy of being fed in ways that lift me up and enhance my life. Today I am making a decision to sweep away the crumbs and realize my own strength.

For anyone who is struggling to let go of the hand that feeds you crumbs, know that there's someone out there who will provide you with a gourmet meal. There's someone out there for every one of us and we don't have to settle for crumbs.

Age: 26

I'm afraid to welcome another birthday
To embrace another year alive,
Because there is something missing—
Deep down inside.

About the Author

Mark Travis Rivera is an award-winning activist and the founder and artistic director of marked dance project (markeddanceproject.com), a contemporary dance company featuring both disabled and nondisabled dancers. In addition, he is a choreographer, dancer, public speaker, and writer.

Rivera works in New York City and lives in New Jersey. More information on his many projects is available at www.MarkTravisRivera.com. Follow him on Twitter @MarkTravRivera.

Made in the USA
Monee, IL
31 March 2022